The Bayer Color Atlas of
Hypertension

Volume 2

The Bayer Color Atlas of
Hypertension

Volume 2

Peter F. Semple

The Medical Research Council Blood Pressure Unit
Western Infirmary, Glasgow

and

George B. M. Lindop

University Department of Pathology
Western Infirmary, Glasgow

Bayer

**Pharmaceutical
Division**

Printed and bound in Spain by T.G. Hostench, S.A.

The volumes in the Series are adapted from a volume under the title *An Atlas of Hypertension* in *The Encyclopedia of Visual Medicine Series* published by The Parthenon Publishing Group.

This edition is published for Bayer Corporation, Pharmaceutical Division by The Parthenon Publishing Group (New York and London) in association with Caduceus Medical Publishers Inc., Patterson, NY, USA.

Bayer

**Pharmaceutical
Division**

Bayer Corporation
400 Morgan Lane
West Haven, CT 06516-4175

Dear Doctor:

To further enhance your reference collection, we are pleased to provide you with Volume II of the new 3-volume *Bayer Color Atlas of Hypertension* by Drs. Semple and Lindop of the University of Glasgow.

Volume II focuses on investigations in renovascular hypertension, renal hypertension and the adrenal cortex, featuring more than thirty photographs and illustrations. As with Volume I, the information contained herein can be a valuable adjunct to your diagnostic skills, and may be helpful in assisting with your patient communication.

We hope you will find Volume II as interesting and informative a contribution to cardiovascular medicine as the first in this three-volume series.

Sincerely,

H. Brian Allen, MD, FFPM
Director, Scientific Relations
     and Health Care Communications

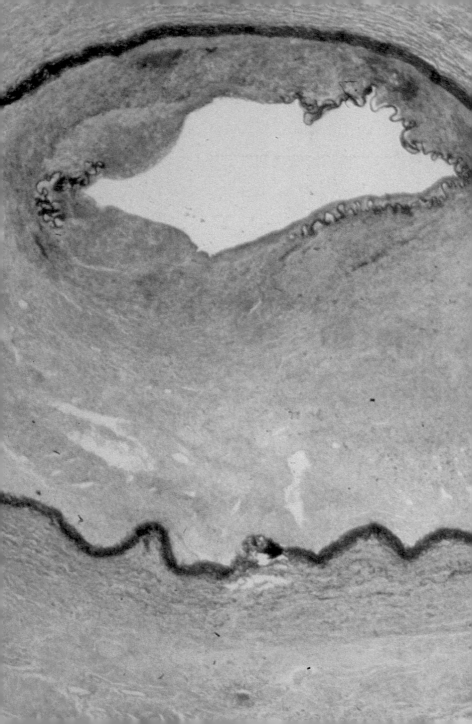

Contents

Measurement of blood pressure

For routine clinical purposes, the mercury sphygmo-manometer is the most reliable and accurate instrument for indirect measurement of blood pressure. Measurements with aneroid sphygmomanomcters may also be accurate but these instruments should be checked at least once a year against a mercury instrument. This can be done by means of a Y-connection between the tubing of the two instruments, with comparisons then made at several levels of pressure. Many of the electronic machines which are marketed for self-measurement of blood pressure are inaccurate and perform poorly when tested against a conventional mercury instrument.

Direct intra-arterial blood pressure measurements in ambulatory subjects studied over 24 hours are made in some centers. This has shown that there is a marked diurnal variation in arterial pressure, with low values during sleep and peak values in the early morning. The peak incidence of cerebral infarction and ischemic stroke coincides with this trough of pressure at night, and the peak incidence of intracranial hemorrhage occurs during periods of high pressure in the daytime. Studies with both direct and indirect ambulatory techniques in hypertension have shown that average values of pressure are generally increased throughout the 24 hours. The significance of a finding of increased variability without a change in average values in terms either of sustained hypertension or of vascular events is not well understood.

The correlation between ambulatory blood pressure measurements and left ventricular mass measured by echocardiography may be closer than the correlation between clinic pressures and ventricular mass. Ambulatory recordings of pressure tend also to resemble self-measured pressures at home, rather than pressures recorded at clinic, office or outpatient departments. An average ambulatory blood pressure greater than 130/85 mmHg over 24 hours is probably abnormal but, as with all methods defining hypertension, this cut-off point is arbitrary. It is important that indirect methods of monitoring ambulatory pressures are carefully validated against intra-arterial methods.

There are some important points to observe if accurate measurements are to be obtained with a conventional mercury sphygmomanometer. The first relates to cuff size. The conventional cuff contains a bladder that is 22 cm in length, which is probably not long enough for routine use and unsatisfactory in patients with obese or well muscled upper arms. If such a bladder is used, it is essential to position the center of the cuff accurately over the brachial artery. It is the recommendation of the British Hypertension Society that the cuff for routine use should contain a bladder that encircles at least 80% of most arms. A cuff which is 35 cm in length meets this specification and is preferred for routine use. In very obese or muscular arms, a bladder that is 42 cm in length should be chosen. For children over 5 years the cuff should contain a bladder that is 12 cm in length. Cuff width is less important than length but width should be about 40% of arm circumference. Cuffs that are wider than 13 cm are not often required in clinical practice.

The following are the most common problems with the mercury sphygmomanometer: there may have been loss of mercury so that the meniscus is not at zero when the cuff is deflated. Black deposits of oxidized mercury on the inner surface of the glass may build up and obscure the meniscus from view. Another common problem is a leak in the system, so that the rate of descent of the column of mercury is greater than 2 mm/s. It should always be possible to inflate the bladder to a pressure greater than 200 mmHg in less than 5 seconds. Cuffs that employ Velcro may wear out so that there is poor apposition of the bladder to the arm.

Some points about technique are worth emphasizing. Measurements of standing pressure that are taken with the arm dependent may give results 5–10 mmHg higher than those obtained with the upper arm supported at heart level. At the initial clinical assessment of a patient with high blood pressure, measurements should be made in both arms sequentially and differences between the arms that are greater than 20/10 mmHg should prompt simultaneous measurement in both arms with two instruments. The arm that gives higher values should be noted and used for subsequent monitoring of pressure.

For clinical trials, the Hawksley random-zero sphygmomanometer is often used and this machine contains a device which muddles the zero and reduces observer bias. Recently, there has been some discussion about possible systematic but small differences in pressure between this instrument and the conventional mercury sphygmomanometer, with slightly lower values obtained with the random-zero instrument. As with ordinary machines, regular maintenance is necessary to ensure that the mercury content and accuracy of the instrument are maintained.

Pressures should be recorded to the nearest 2 mmHg. In most circumstances, the diastolic pressure is measured at phase 5 Korotkoff, which is the point at which sounds disappear. If there is a wide pulse pressure due to aortic regurgitation, thyrotoxicosis or muscle vasodilatation, then phase 5 may continue to 0 mmHg. In that event, the diastolic should be recorded at phase 4 (muffling of the sounds) and labelled as such. The hemodynamic changes in pregnancy cause disappearance of phase 5 Korotkoff, and in pregnant patients phase 4 may be preferred. If the brachial or radial artery remains palpable distal to a point when the artery is occluded manually or by a cuff (Osler's maneuver), then measurements of blood pressure by the indirect method may overestimate the intra-arterial pressure. This most often arises in elderly subjects with reduced arterial compliance caused by arteriosclerosis, and has been described as 'pseudohypertension'.

Investigation of secondary hypertension

Renovascular hypertension

Renovascular hypertension is generally uncommon if sought in asymptomatic individuals with mild-to-moderate hypertension in early adult and middle life. Routine screening for the condition is seldom offered, although raised lev els of plasma renin activity in hypertensives who are taking a diet of normal sodium content may identify a subset of patients in whom further investigation is appropriate. The prevalence figures in cross-sectional surveys may not give an adequate view of the problem, since atheromatous renal artery disease quite often develops in individuals with long-standing primary hypertension and other risk factors for atherosclerosis such as cigarette smoking or high blood levels of cholesterol. The prevalence of renovascular disease increases with age and runs parallel to the increase in incidence of atheromatous disease of the abdominal aorta.

Angioplasty now offers a less-invasive approach to treatment than renal artery surgery, although re-stenosis is increasingly recognized. Angioplasty also carries a particular risk of compromising renal function in patients with extensive atheromatous disease.

Detection of renovascular disease has become more important since the introduction of angiotensin-converting enzyme inhibitors, because inadvertent treatment of affected patients with these drugs may cause deterioration in renal function. This may be severe and clinically important if there is bilateral disease and where extracellular fluid volume has been depleted by treatment with potent diuretics such as frusemide.

The following groups of patients are at high risk of atheromatous renal artery stenosis. About 30% of patients with established peripheral vascular disease have coincident unilateral renal artery stenosis and about 10% have bilateral disease. Stenoses may be bilateral or there may be stenosis on one side with occlusion of the renal artery on the contralateral side. Patients with abdominal aortic aneurysms quite often have renovascular disease, and patients with hypertension and atheromatous carotid artery stenosis show an increased incidence. Older patients (> 60 years) with high blood pressure and impairment of renal function are a group with a high prevalence of atheromatous renal artery disease. Deterioration of renal function after treatment with an angiotensin-converting enzyme inhibitor has already been mentioned. Another context in which atheromatous disease should be sought is where there is a sudden and unexplained deterioration in control of blood pressure using drugs. A group at high risk are patients with malignant or accelerated hypertension, particularly if bilateral retinal hemorrhages develop on drug treatment or if the condition presents after the age of 50 years.

In patients under the age of 40 years, renovascular disease is much less common but is sometimes seen in women with severe hypertension who have fibromuscular dysplasia. This rare condition should be suspected if a woman develops severe hypertension without any family history of high blood pressure or stroke. There are usually high or high-normal levels of plasma renin activity in the untreated state, and rapid normalization of blood pressure after treatment with an angiotensin-converting enzyme inhibitor is often observed. Fibromuscular dysplasia can be identified on angiography as a characteristic beaded segment of artery where areas of arterial narrowing are interspersed with intervening areas of arterial dilatation. The radiological appearance is sometimes described as similar to a 'string of beads'. Disease may be localized to the renal arteries but may also affect other larger arteries such as the mesenterics. The cause is not established, but cigarette smoking may be a risk factor. The response of arterial pressure to revascularization by angioplasty or surgery is usually excellent, providing that technical success has been achieved. Normalization or substantial improvement in blood pressure is usual. This contrasts quite markedly with the response rate in atheromatous renal artery disease where cure is much less frequent. Factors that tend to predict a poor response are overall impairment of renal function or long duration of hypertension.

Digital subtraction angiography is a relatively non-invasive way of visualizing the renal arteries and obviates the need to puncture an artery. Cardiac disease and reduced left ventricular function may impair the quality of the angiogram after such intravenous injections of contrast. Isotope renography alone using [^{123}I]hippuran, [^{99}Tc]MAG3 or ^{99}[Tc]DTPA is not a particularly sensitive screening method for unilateral renal artery stenosis, but renography after acute treatment with captopril does improve the sensitivity of the technique and can also give useful information about the functional significance of a lesion suspected from angiography.

After positive angiography or captopril renography, the next step in unilateral renal artery stenosis is the measurement of levels of renin in renal venous blood. This technique is most sensitive if bilateral simultaneous samples are taken from the renal veins, together with samples from a peripheral vein, which should be the same as levels in arterial blood. About three samples from each site are sufficient. The main factor that determines the renal vein renin ratio is renal blood flow rather than increased secretion rate of renin. Suppression of renin secretion from the contralateral kidney may also be sought. Discrepancies between levels of renin in renal venous blood from two kidneys may occur in patients who have had severe or malignant hypertension, and probably result from asymmetric damage to small arteries and arterioles.

Patients with bilateral renovascular disease, and particularly those with severe abdominal atheroma and stenosis at the origin of the renal artery or arteries, tend to show disappointing responses to surgery. This type of patient often has atheromatous disease in the coronary circulation and the extracranial carotid system, and there are appreciable risks of myocardial or cerebral infarction in the perioperative period. Duplex ultrasound examination of the carotid arteries may be contemplated in this high-risk group, particularly if reconstructive surgery is to be attempted. Coronary artery disease may also require investigation and treatment. This difficult group of patients with advanced disease do not respond well to angioplasty. Arterial catheterization of atheromatous renal vessels and aorta may cause embolism of cholesterol-rich debris, with resultant deterioration of renal function (renal arteries), abdominal pain (mesenteric vessels) and/or livedo reticularis (limb vessels). Renal artery occlusion due to thrombosis superimposed on atheromatous plaque may lead to complete loss of renal function, unless a collateral circulation has developed during a period of progressive arterial narrowing. In younger patients with fibromuscular disease, arterial dissection may occur with thrombosis and present as flank pain with micro- or macroscopic hematuria and hypertension. This complication, although rare, is well recognized.

Renal hypertension

Many primary renal diseases that cause chronic impairment of kidney function lead to high blood pressure. Left ventricular hypertrophy is common and often present in patients maintained on hemodialysis, despite treatment with antihypertensive drugs. Hypertension frequently develops in patients with glomerulonephritis, and the most common variety that is encountered in blood pressure clinics is IgA nephropathy or Berger's disease. Microscopic hematuria and modest proteinuria are usually the first clue to the diagnosis in patients who do not have these changes as a result of severe or malignant hypertension. The condition is so called because immunocytochemistry of renal tissue showed that mesangial deposition of IgA is a dominant feature. Hematuria is usually microscopic, although intermittent frank hematuria is not uncommon. Although there is accumulating evidence for relentless progression into chronic renal failure in a proportion of these patients, the rapidity of this progression varies greatly, with a small proportion of patients maintaining normal renal function for many years after diagnosis.

In patients with chronic renal failure, high blood pressure is caused by a combination of volume expansion due to retention of sodium and water, and activation of the renin–angiotensin system. Unless extracellular fluid volume is controlled by dialysis, then adequate natriuresis requires use of loop-diuretic drugs such as frusemide, which may require to be given in large doses. Restriction of dietary sodium intake to around 50 mmol/day may be a helpful adjunct to diuretic treatment. Thiazide diuretics are not effective except in the very early stages of renal impairment. In patients on dialysis treatment, blood pressure control is more readily achieved with the continuous ambulatory peritoneal technique than with intermittent peritoneal dialysis or hemodialysis. Erythropoietin treatment of anemia tends to increase arterial pressure in parallel with the rise in hematocrit and blood viscosity.

Chronic renal disease is the most common cause of high blood pressure in children and young adults and may also cause severe of malignant hypertension. In girls, reflux-nephropathy is an important cause of high blood pressure, which may present as severe or malignant hypertension up to the age of about 20 years. Disease is often bilateral, but unilateral reflux with renal scarring and unilateral renin secretion is sometimes found. Hypertension may then be cured or greatly improved by nephrectomy, providing that there is an adequate function in the remaining kidney. Mild high blood pressure in children or young adults may be due to primary hypertension, but investigation to exclude renal disease is often appropriate in this young age group. The rate of rise in blood pressure in adolescence is particularly marked in the obese.

Adrenal cortex
Primary aldosteronism
Primary aldosteronism or Conn's syndrome is a much less common cause of high blood pressure compared with reno-

vascular hypertension and most often affects women. Hypokalemia may cause symptoms of weakness and polyuria but the condition is usually first suspected after routine measurement of concentrations of plasma electrolytes has shown hypokalemia, often accompanied by a slight increase in the serum concentration of sodium. Paralysis of skeletal muscle caused by severe hypokalemia has sometimes been seen if a patient with primary hyperaldosteronism has been treated with a thiazide or loop diuretic or takes a very high dietary intake of sodium. There is then increased delivery of sodium to the distal tubular exchange site where mineralocorticoid receptors are located.

Hypokalemia due to diuretic treatment is more common than is hypokalemia due to primary aldosteronism, but then is often associated with normal or slightly subnormal serum concentrations of sodium. Measurement of plasma renin activity offers a better method of discrimination. Patients with primary aldosteronism have marked suppression of plasma renin activity or concentration unless treated with a diuretic or taking a diet of low sodium content: volume depletion caused by thiazides causes activation of the renin–angiotensin system. The confounding effect of a diet of low sodium content may be excluded by measuring urinary excretion of sodium over 24 hours. Patients with malignant or accelerated hypertension and a few patients with renovascular hypertension develop hypokalemia, due to high levels of aldosterone caused by angiotensin II and driven by high levels of plasma renin activity. Hypokalemia and hyperaldosteronism due to angiotensin are corrected by treatment with an angiotensin converting enzyme (ACE) inhibitor, but hypokalemia and high levels of aldosterone will persist if there is primary aldosteronism. Plasma renin activity also remains suppressed.

A diagnosis of primary aldosteronism is confirmed if there are high plasma concentrations of aldosterone in morning samples or increased urinary aldosterone excretion with marked suppression of plasma renin activity. An anomalous postural fall in plasma levels of aldosterone is sometimes present. In primary aldosteronism, the plasma concentrations of aldosterone follow the diurnal rhythm of adrenocorticotropin hormone (ACTH) secretion so that a component of the fall observed after ambulation between 08 00 and 12 00 may be due to the fall in ACTH. In cases of difficulty, measurements of the 18-hydroxylated steroids 18-hydroxycorticosterone and 18-hydroxycortisol may be helpful. The finding of raised levels of 18-hydroxycortisol suggests that there is autonomous secretion of aldosterone, and levels of both corticosteroids are less likely to be modified by hypokalemia than levels of aldosterone. Low plasma renin activity accompanied by low concentrations of aldosterone point to hypertension caused by another mineralocorticoid, either self-administered or endogenous: some of the syndromes due to inherited deficiencies of enzymes of corticosteroid biosynthesis give rise to mineralocorticoid hypertension caused by ACTH and characterized by high plasma levels of deoxycorticosterone.

Once a biochemical diagnosis of primary aldosteronism is established, it is then appropriate to attempt to localize an adenoma. Lesions are often demonstrated by computed tomography but tumors less than 1.5 cm in diameter may not be visualized. The technique does not distinguish large non-functioning nodules from aldosteronomas. Most lesions are less than 3 cm in diameter and beyond the resolution of ultrasound scanning. If a tumor greater than 3 cm in diameter is identified, then malignancy may be suspected. Malignant adrenal tumors seldom present with mineralocorticoid hypertension and rarely, if ever, synthesize aldosterone. A few secrete other mineralocorticoids such as deoxycorticosterone.

If an adenoma is suspected, then adrenal vein catheterization with measurements of aldosterone in adrenal venous blood, collected without suction from a syringe, is the most accurate way of confirming or establishing the diagnosis before surgery. This can be difficult on the right side. Contrast injection into an adrenal vein may cause infarction of the gland. Venography has been used in some centers in the past, but has been less used since the advent of computed tomography. Seleno- or iodo-cholesterol scintigraphy, after a period of dexamethasone pretreatment, has sometimes been useful but the false-negative rate is high and the method has not found general favor.

A small proportion of patients (10–20%) have idiopathic aldosteronism without evidence of adenoma, but a tumor cannot be excluded with confidence unless aldosterone has been measured in samples of adrenal venous blood. Differentiation of idiopathic aldosteronism from low-renin essential hypertension can be difficult. About 30% of patients with essential hypertension have low levels of renin activity, and a subgroup have mildly raised aldosterone levels.

In primary aldosteronism, preoperative treatment with the potassium-sparing diuretic amiloride (10–50 mg/day) corrects extracellular fluid volume expansion, reduces pressure and normalizes serum potassium. The response of blood pressure to this correction of body sodium predicts the blood pressure response to surgery. Sodium space or total exchangeable sodium measured by isotopic dilution is between 105% and 120% of normal in untreated adenoma patients, and falls to 100% or less after drug treatment or surgery. Plasma renin activity may be used as an index of extracellular fluid volume status during drug treatment and as a guide to the dose of amiloride. The dose of drug that controls pressure tends to reduce exchangeable sodium below normal, and this probably reflects the relatively high prevalence of residual hypertension after surgery. Blood pressure after surgery is probably only normalized in about 50% of patients. Patients with impaired renal function are likely to have a less satisfactory blood pressure response. Extracellular volume expansion due to mineralocorticoid excess normally causes an increase in glomerular filtration rate so that creatinine clearance usually falls after medical or surgical treatment. An alternative to amiloride is the aldosterone antagonist spironolactone, which may be used in doses of up to 300 mg/day. With spironolactone there is a significant incidence of side-effects and some concern about the potential for the drug to cause breast cancer. Long-term use of spironolactone is no longer recommended.

Other forms of mineralocorticoid hypertension There are syndromes caused by deficiency of enzymes involved in cortisol biosynthesis, such as 17α-hydroxylase deficiency and 11β-hydroxylase deficiency, which cause mineralocorticoid hypertension. 17α-hydroxylase deficiency is accompanied by failure of sexual development because the enzyme is necessary for synthesis of the sex steroids. 11β-hydroxylase deficiency is accompanied by virilization in females or precocious puberty in males. In both syndromes, decreased cortisol secretion releases ACTH from feedback inhibition, and ACTH then stimulates excessive secretion of the mineralocorticoid deoxycorticosterone from the adrenal cortex. A further very rare enzyme deficiency is 11β-hydroxy-steroid dehydrogenase deficiency, where cortisol-to-cortisone metabolism within the kidney and other tissues is reduced, thereby increasing concentrations of cortisol locally. This 'shuttle' enzyme normally protects the mineralocorticoid receptor from interacting with circulating cortisol. Liquorice and the drug carbenoxolone sodium inhibit the dehydrogenase and probably exert their mineralocorticoid effects via this mechanism.

Cushing's syndrome

Hypertension occurs frequently in Cushing's syndrome, although the mechanism is not as clearly understood as in primary aldosteronism. Hypertension is perhaps most frequent in ACTH-mediated disease such as pituitary-dependent Cushing's disease or the syndrome of ectopic ACTH secretion from a carcinoid tumor. Several factors may be involved in pathogenesis including activation of Type I (mineralocorticoid) and Type II (glucocorticoid) receptors by cortisol, and production of other hypertensinogenic steroids from the adrenal cortex. Hypokalemia tends only to be seen if ACTH levels are particularly high in the ectopic syndromes. Cushing's syndrome due to an adrenal adenoma (or carcinoma) is relatively uncommon (about 10% of cases).

Hypertension in pituitary-dependent Cushing's disease usually responds to curative transsphenoidal hypophysectomy. Otherwise, patients with Cushing's syndrome and hypertension should be treated with conventional antihypertensive drugs, although non-potassium-sparing diuretics are probably best avoided.

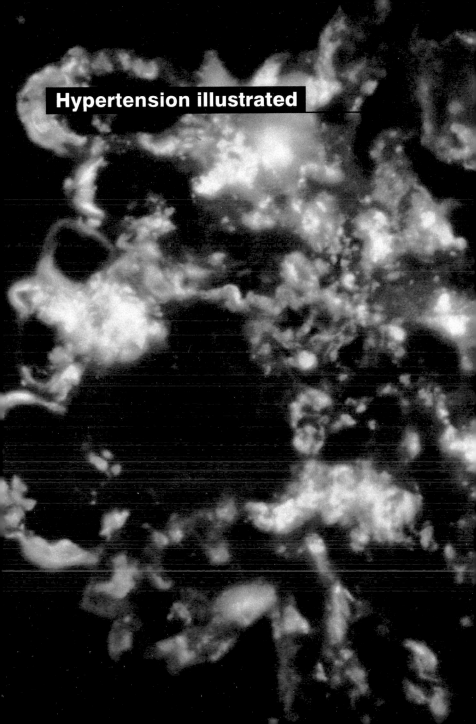

Hypertension illustrated

List of illustrations

Figure 16
Angiogram of renal artery dissection
Figure 17
Dissection of fibromuscular dysplasia
Figure 18
Renogram in renovascular hypertension
Figure 19
Renal artery stenosis
Figure 20
Urography in renovascular hypertension
Figure 21
Renal artery stenosis – before treatment
Figure 22
Renal artery stenosis – after treatment
Figure 23
Atrophy caused by stenosis of a polar artery
Figure 24
Renin in ischemic and normal kidney
Figure 25
Bilateral atheromatous disease
Figure 26
Atheroma of the aorta
Figure 27
Aortic atheroma causing renal artery stenosis
Figure 28
Cholesterol embolism
Figure 29
Occluded renal arteries
Figure 30
Capsular collaterals
Figure 31
Polyarteritis nodosa
Figure 32
IgA nephritis

Figure 1 A small renal artery and arteriole both affected by arteriolosclerosis. The smooth muscle cells of the media are replaced by homogeneous pink deposits of glycoprotein stained magenta with a PAS stain. This material, which comprises both protein derived from the plasma and synthesized matrix protein, causes thickening and narrowing of the arterioles and small arteries in chronic hypertension

Figure 2 A renal interlobular artery with arteriosclerosis, and stained to show elastic tissue. There is considerable intimal thickening due to fibrosis with reduplication of the internal elastic lamina and atrophy of the media. Similar changes occur in old age

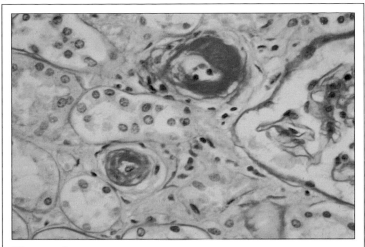

Figure 1

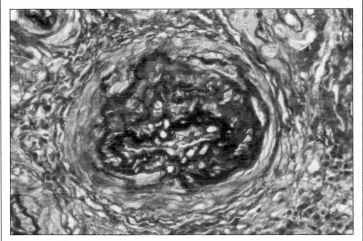

Figure 2

Figure 3 A section of kidney from a patient with severe hypertension. The MSB stain shows that one of the three sections of arteriole has media that is thickened by red-staining 'fibrinoid', which results from insudation of plasma proteins such as fibrinogen and fibrin. Proteins gain entry because the permeability of the vessel is increased in response to damage from very high intraluminal pressures

Figure 4 The typical appearance of the kidneys in malignant-phase hypertension. The kidneys are swollen and edematous. The renal capsule has been peeled off to show tiny punctate hemorrhages on the surface – the so-called 'flea-bitten' kidney

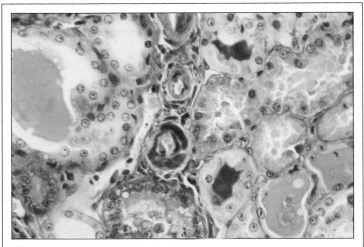

Figure 3

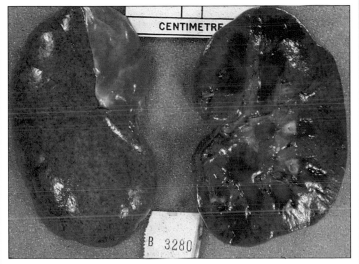

Figure 4

Figure 5 Blood film appearances from a patient with malignant or accelerated hypertension. There is red-cell fragmentation with helmet cells and spherocytes typical of microangiopathic hemolytic anemia. The platelet count is usually low

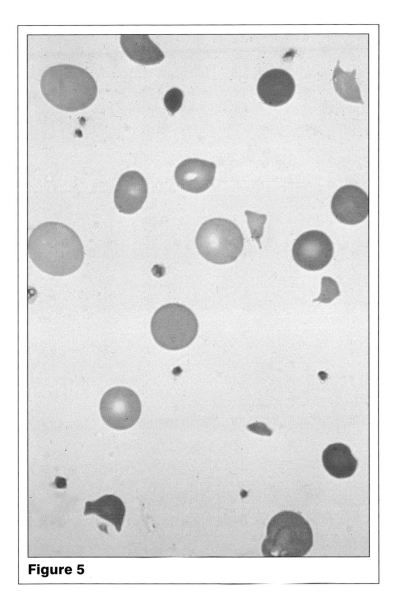

Figure 5

Figure 6 A section of kidney from a patient with malignant hypertension. Masson's trichrome shows red areas of fibrinoid. Two vessels show fibrinoid necrosis and intravascular coagulation. The remaining terminal interlobular artery shows 'onion skin' proliferative endarteritis. This is probably a healing response to acute injury

Figure 7 The granular surface of the kidneys from a patient who died some years after treatment of malignant hypertension. This appearance is due to ischemic scarring caused by proliferative endarteritis in the healing phase of severe hypertension. Prognosis in treated malignant hypertension is related to initial renal function rather than height of pressure

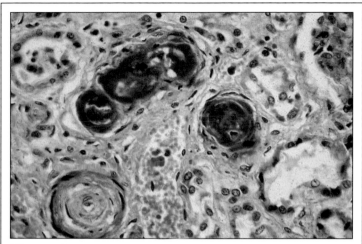

Figure 6

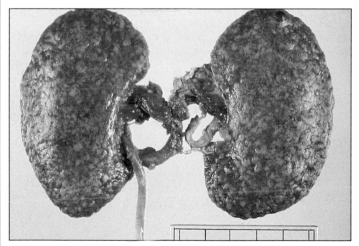

Figure 7

Figure 8 The mercury sphygmomanometer remains the 'gold standard' method of measuring arterial pressure by the indirect method. All who measure blood pressures should undergo a short period of formal training. One point which is illustrated shows the correct position of the arm, which is supported at heart level

Figure 9 Common remediable causes of inaccuracy are: (1) the mercury meniscus does not start at zero; (2) the inside of the tubing is dirty; (3) the valve is not functioning correctly. There should not be any leak when the valve is closed and the rate of descent of the mercury meniscus should be able to be adjusted to 2 mm/s or less

Figure 10 Bladders of three different sizes are shown. The standard cuff for blood pressure measurement should contain a bladder that is 35 cm in length (middle), which is longer than the traditional 22 cm bladder (lower). If the 22 cm cuff is used then it is very important to place the center of the cuff accurately over the brachial artery. If the bladder is too short for an obese arm then the pressure will be overestimated

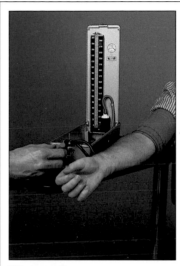

Figure 8

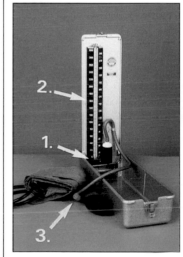

Figure 9

Figure 10

Figure 11 An arteriogram from a patient with normal aorta and renal arteries

Figure 12 A histological section of fibromuscular dysplasia of the renal artery cut longitudinally and showing distortion of the media by bands of fibromuscular tissue with intervening areas of thinning. The thickened areas cause stenosis and the thinned areas may give rise to aneurysms

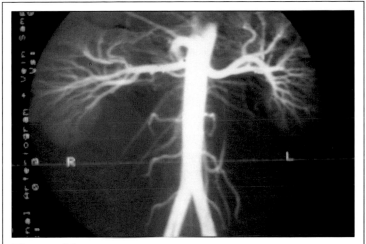

Figure 11

Figure 12

Figure 13 A photomicrograph showing a normal juxtaglomerular apparatus. The section has been stained with a renin antiserum and an immunoperoxidase technique which stains the renin granules brown. The positive-staining cells are in the afferent and efferent arterioles at the root of the glomerulus

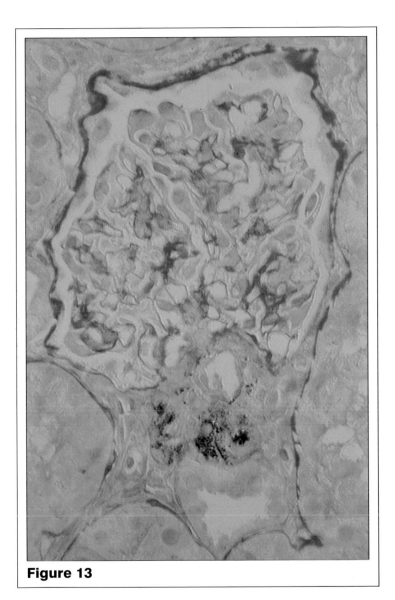

Figure 13

Figure 14 An angiogram showing a renal artery stenosis due to fibromuscular dysplasia. There are alternating areas of constriction and dilatation – the so-called 'string of beads' appearance

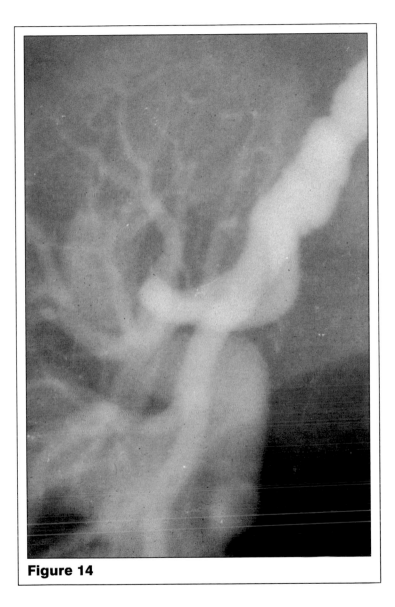

Figure 14

Figure 15 This juxtaglomerular apparatus is from a kidney with renal artery stenosis. There is considerable increase in the number of renin-secreting cells, both in the afferent and efferent arterioles: positive staining extends into the extraglomerular mesangium. The renin-secreting cells are greatly increased in size. The increase in number of cells is thought to arise from metaplasia

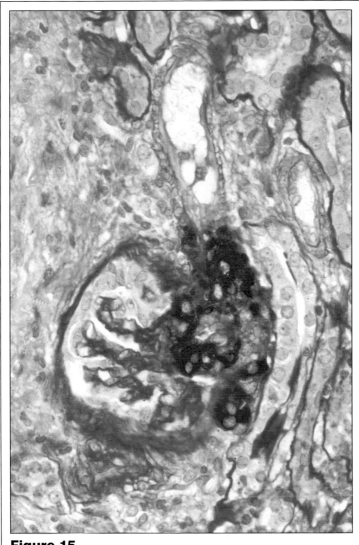

Figure 15

Figure 16 There has been dissection and thrombosis of a segment of fibromuscular hyperplasia of the right renal artery in this young woman, who presented with loin pain and hypertension

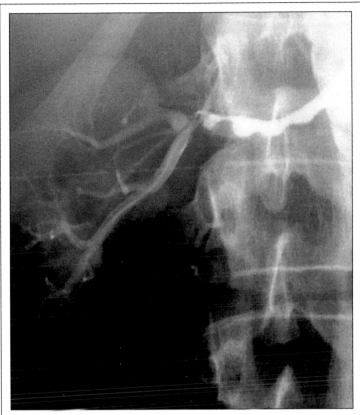

Figure 16

Figure 17 A transverse section through a renal artery which is stained to show elastic fibers black. This is the typical appearance of the perimedial type of fibromuscular dysplasia. The internal elastic lamina is seen as a black line which is fragmented. Some residual media is enclosed by the thicker external elastic lamina. Below and to the left is a hematoma (reddish-brown) caused by a dissection

Figure 18 [^{123}I]hippuran renogram showing the curves of radioactivity from over the kidneys of the same patient. Over the affected kidney the vascular phase is delayed and the washout phase is prolonged. The peak of radioactivity is also reduced. Renography after a single dose of captopril is a good method of detecting functional unilateral renal artery stenosis

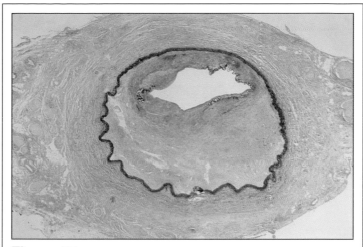

Figure 17

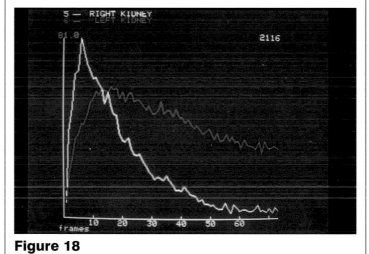

Figure 18

Figure 19 A short segment of fibromuscular hyperplasia causing renal artery stenosis in a young woman with severe hypertension

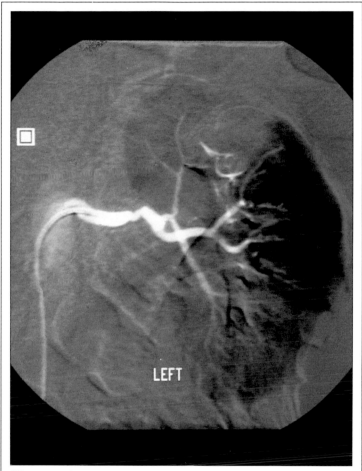

Figure 19

Figure 20 Intravenous urogram from the same patient as in Figure 19 showing increased density of contrast in the collecting system of the affected kidney (left) which is then slow to washout after an oral water load. Kidney size may be reduced (not obvious in this instance). In very severe stenosis, appearance of contrast on the affected side may be delayed. Urography has been largely superseded by captopril renography or digital subtraction angiography

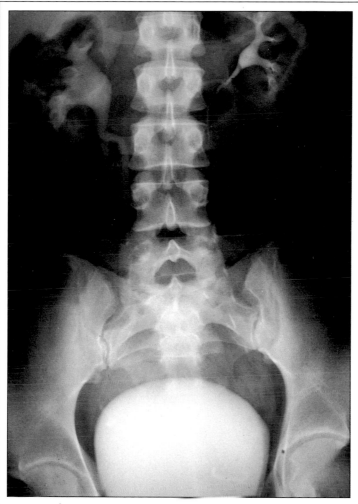

Figure 20

Figure 21 Selective arteriogram of a right renal artery in a woman with hypertension showing a tight and localized stenosis due to fibromuscular hyperplasia

Figure 22 The same stenosis after successful balloon angioplasty. Treatment of renovascular hypertension due to fibromuscular hyperplasia is more likely to result in cure and improvement of hypertension than is treatment of atheromatous lesions

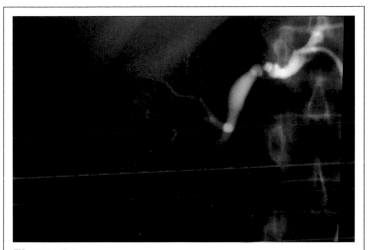

Figure 21

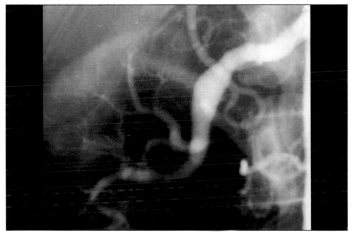

Figure 22

Figure 23 The typical appearance of a kidney affected by stenosis of an artery supplying the lower pole. The lower part of the kidney is shrunken and has contracted below the level of the normal kidney. It is darker red and more granular than adjacent normal kidney

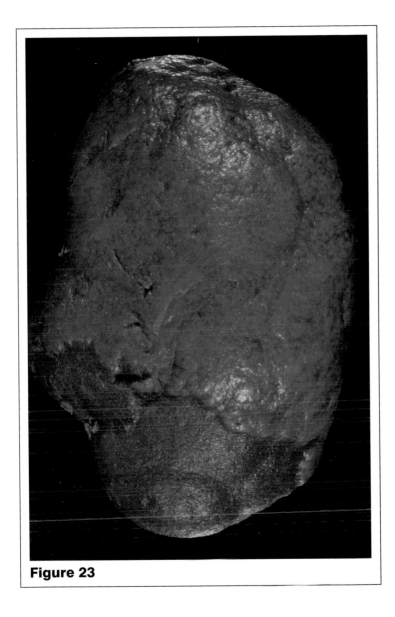

Figure 23

Figure 24 The junction of ischemic renal cortex (right) and the normal cortex (left). The immunoperoxidase technique shows abundant immunostainable renin (brown) in hyperplastic juxtaglomerular apparatuses in the ischemic area. There is diminished renin in the normal kidney due to suppression of renin synthesis

Figure 25 An aortogram showing severe atheroma with tight stenoses at the origin of both renal arteries. There is prominent poststenotic dilatation on the right. Stenoses of this type are difficult to treat with angioplasty or surgery, and there is an appreciable risk of sudden deterioration of renal function following treatment with angiotensin converting enzyme inhibitors. The chance of renal failure is further increased by treatment with loop diuretics

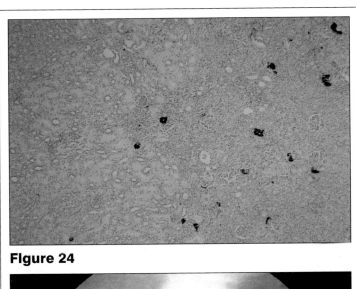

Figure 24

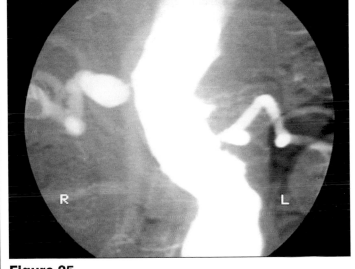

Figure 25

Figure 26 An aorta removed at autopsy. There is severe atheroma especially in the lower portion and the iliac arteries. Just below the origins of the renal arteries is a large saccular aneurysm filled with thrombus. Aortic aneurysms are common in men with hypertension over 60 years of age

Figure 27 A close-up view of the aorta with a portion of vena cava behind. The aorta has been opened posteriorly to show the origins of the superior mesenteric artery and both renal arteries. The origin of the right renal artery (indicated by an arrow) is narrowed by an ulcerated atheromatous plaque. If such a plaque ulcerates, then thrombosis and renal infarction may ensue

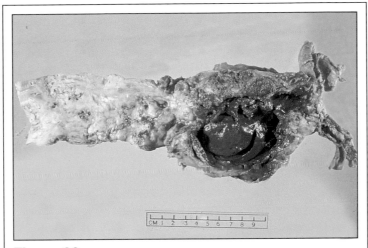

Figure 26

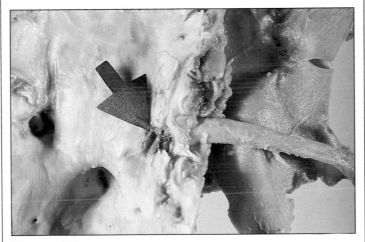

Figure 27

Figure 28 A medium-sized artery occluded by atheromatous debris and thrombus. The slit-like spaces are caused by cholesterol crystals from a ruptured atheromatous plaque, probably situated in the aorta. Arteriography or angioplasty in patients with extensive atheroma may also cause cholesterol embolism, resulting in deterioration of renal function, abdominal pain or livedo reticularis

Figure 29 A patient who presented with acute renal failure after administration of an angiotensin-converting enzyme (ACE) inhibitor. There is occlusion of both main renal arteries with some blood flow to the kidneys maintained via collateral vessels. Renal failure after ACE inhibitor treatment is usually reversible. A causal relationship between drug treatment and renal artery occlusion has not been established

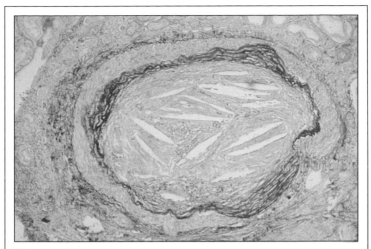

Figure 28

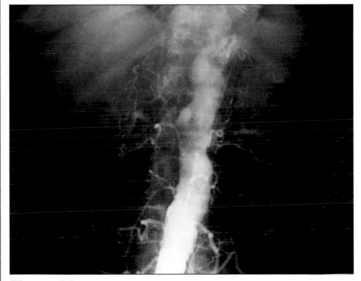

Figure 29

Figure 30 In chronic renal artery stenosis or renal artery occlusion, collateral vessels may develop from capsular and periureteric vessels. This angiogram shows prominent capsular collaterals in a young man with long-standing renal artery occlusion due to neurofibromatosis

Figure 31 Angiogram of the right kidney (upper panels) and a hepatic artery (lower panels) from a man with polyarteritis nodosa. There are multiple small aneurysms. Polyarteritis usually occurs in men and tends to present with hypertension associated with fever, abdominal pain, leukocytosis and evidence of impairment of renal function

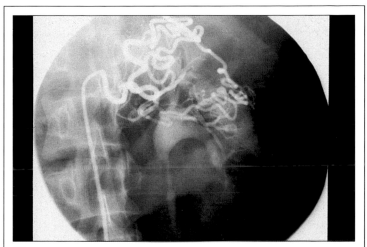

Figure 30

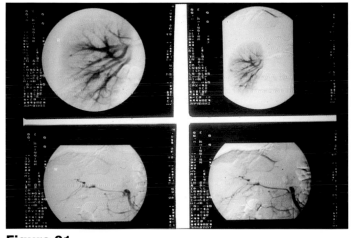

Figure 31

Figure 32 A photomicrograph of a renal glomerulus. The immunofluorescence technique shows bright granular fluorescent deposits of IgA immune complexes deposited largely in the mesangium. The appearances are typical of IgA nephropathy (Berger's syndrome). Patients with IgA nephropathy commonly present with hypertension and usually show positive urine stick tests for blood and protein

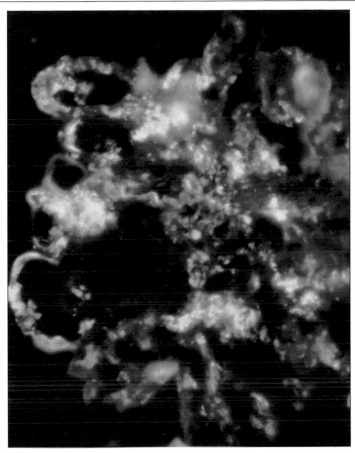

Figure 32

Acknowledgements

Drs Patricia Morley, Andrew Morris, Henry Dargie, James McLenachan, Jehoida Brown, John Connell, Andrew Collier, John Kingdom, Ian More, Amir Azmy and Mr Gerard Hillen all contributed slides and the authors thank them.

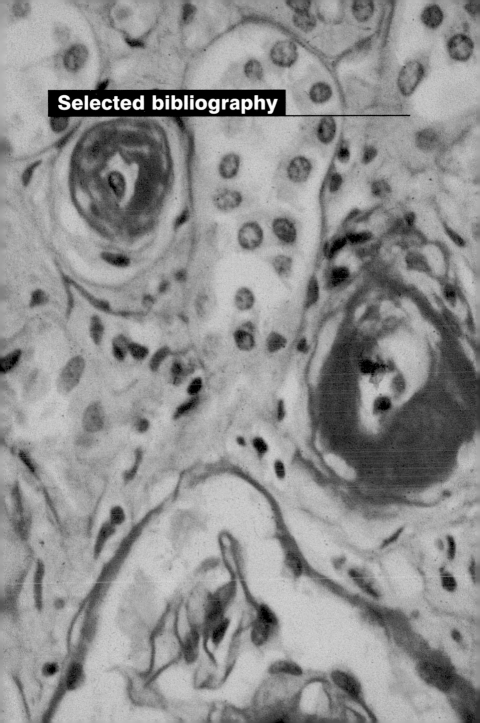

Selected bibliography

Measurement of blood pressure

Petrie, J. C., O'Brien, E. T., Littler, W. A. and de Swiet, M. (1986). British Hypertension Society. Recommendations on blood pressure measurement. *Br. Med. J.*, **293**, 611–15

Pickering, T. G., Harshfield, G. A., Kleinert, H. D. *et al.* (1982). Comparisons of blood pressure during normal daily activities, sleep and exercise in normal and hypertensive subjects. *J. Am. Med. Assoc.*, **247**, 992–6

Pickering, T. G. and Devereux, R. B. (1987). Ambulatory monitoring of blood pressure as a predictor of cardiovascular risk. *Am. Heart J.*, **114**, 925–8

(1991). Ambulatory blood pressure monitoring: clinical issues. *J. Hypertension*, **9** (Suppl. 1), 31–45

Investigation of secondary hypertension

Renal hypertension

D'Amico, G., Barbiano di Belgioioso, G., Bertoli, S. *et al.* (1985). Idiopathic IgA mesangial nephropathy. Clinical and histological study of 374 patients. *Medicine (Baltimore)*, **64**, 49–60

Parfrey, P. S., Bear, J. C., Morgan, J. *et al.* (1990). The diagnosis and prognosis of autosomal dominant polycystic kidney disease. *N. Engl. J. Med.*, **323**, 1085–90

Renovascular hypertension

Simon, N., Franklin, S. S., Bleifer, K. H. and Maxwell, M. H. (1972). Co-operative study of renovascular hypertension: clinical characteristics of renovascular hypertension. *J. Am. Med. Assoc.*, **220**, 1209–18

Pauker, S.G. and Kopelman, R. I. (1989). Screening for renovascular hypertension. A which hunt. *Hypertension*, **14**, 258–60

Geyskes, G., Oei, H. Y., Puylaert, G. B. and Dorhout Mees, E. J. (1987). Renovascular hypertension identified by captopril-induced changes in the renogram. *Hypertension*, **9**, 451–8

Sos, T. A., Pickering, T. G., Sniderman, K. *et al.* (1983). Percutaneous transluminal renal angioplasty in renovascular hypertension due to atheroma or fibromuscular dysplasia. *N. Engl. J. Med.*, **309**, 274–9

Grimm, C. E., Yune, H. Y., Donohue, J. P. *et al.* (1986). Renal vascular hypertension. *Nephron*, **44a** (suppl. 1), 96–100

Ying, C. Y., Tifft, C. P., Gavras, H. and Chobanian, A. V. (1984). Renal revascularization in the azotaemic hypersensitive patient resistant to therapy. *N. Engl. J. Med.*, **311**, 1070–5

Sang, C. N., Whelton, P. K., Hamper, U. M. *et al.* (1989). Etiologic factors in fibromuscular dysplasia. *Hypertension*, **14**, 472–9

Adrenal cortex
Primary aldosteronism
Fraser, R., Davies, D. L. and Connell, J. M. C. (1989). Hormones and hypertension. *Clin. Endocrinol.*, **31**, 701–46
Bigleri, E. G. and Irony, I. (1990). Primary aldosteronism. In Martini, L. (ed.) *Endocrine Hypertension*, pp. 71–85 (New York: Raven Press)

Davies, D. L., McElroy, K., Atkinson, A. B. *et al.* (1979). Relationship between exchangeable sodium and blood pressure in different forms of hypertension in man. *Clin. Sci.*, **57**, 69s–75s

Cushing's syndrome
Whitworth, J. A. (1987). Mechanisms of glucocorticoid-induced hypertension. *Kidney Int.*, **31**, 1213–24

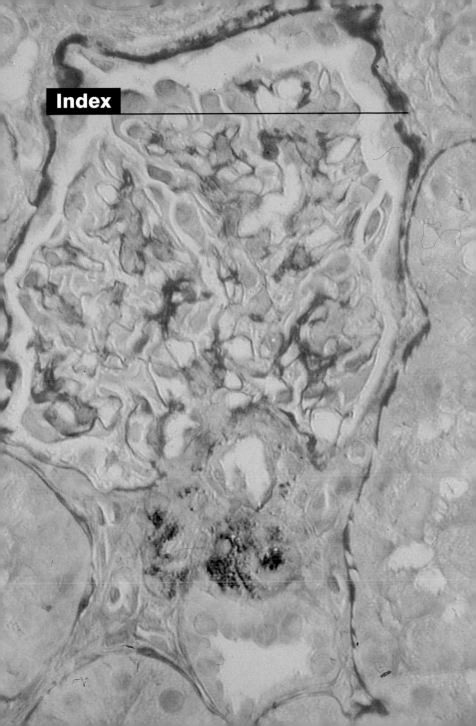

Index

Index

random-zero
sphygmomanometer 11
reflux nephropathy 18
renal arteries
atheroma 58, 59
dissection 46, 46, 48, 49
normal 38, 39
stenosis of 14, 42, 43,
44, 45, 48, 49, 50, 51,
54, 55, 58, 59
surgery on 13
renal disease in children 18
renal hypertension 17
renin
in ischemic kidney 58,
59
in normal kidney 40, 41,
58, 59
in renal artery stenosis 42,
43
plasma in fibromuscular
dysplasia 14
plasma in primary
aldosteronism 9
plasma in primary
hypertension 13
renovascular hypertension
hypokalemia in 19
renogram of 48, 49
urogram of 52, 53
re-stenosis 13
retinal hemorrhages
and renal hypertension
14

bilateral 14

scintigraphy 21
secondary hypertension
13–24
renovascular
hypertension 13
sodium intake 11
and plasma renin activity
13
and primary
aldosteronism 19
sphygmomanometers 9–12,
36, 37
spironolactone 22
stenosis
of carotid artery 14
of renal artery 14, 42,
43, 44, 45, 50, 51, 54,
55, 56
stroke
peak occurrence of 9

thiazide diuretics 18
tumors
adenoma 20, 21

venography of adrenal 21
ventricular hypertrophy
in patients on
hemodialysis 18

Contents of Volume 1

Contents of Volume 1

List of illustrations in Volume 1

Figure 25 Widened
  mediastinum in dissection

Figure 26 Aortic dissection

Figure 27 Degeneration of
  the aortic media

Figure 28 Granular kidney

Figure 29 Nephrosclerosis in
  hypertension

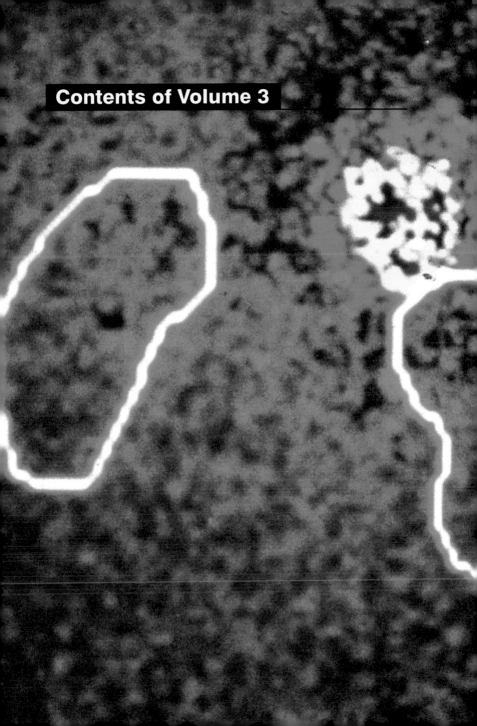

Contents of Volume 3

Contents of Volume 3

List of illustrations in Volume 3

Notes

Notes

Notes

Notes

Notes

ADALAT® CC
(nifedipine)
Extended Release Tablets
For Oral Use

PZ500005

3/95

DESCRIPTION

ADALAT® CC is an extended release tablet dosage form of the calcium channel blocker nifedipine. Nifedipine is 3,5-pyridinedicarboxylic acid, 1,4-dihydro-2,6-dimethyl-4-(2-nitrophenyl)-dimethyl ester, $C_{17}H_{18}N_2O_6$, and has the structural formula:

Nifedipine is a yellow crystalline substance, practically insoluble in water but soluble in ethanol. It has a molecular weight of 346.3. ADALAT CC tablets consist of an external coat and an internal core. Both contain nifedipine, the coat as a slow release formulation and the core as a fast release formulation. ADALAT CC tablets contain either 30, 60, or 90 mg of nifedipine for once-a-day oral administration.

Inert ingredients in the formulation are: hydroxypropylcellulose, lactose, corn starch, crospovidone, microcrystalline cellulose, silicon dioxide, and magnesium stearate. The inert ingredients in the film coating are: hydroxypropylmethylcellulose, polyethylene glycol, ferric oxide, and titanium dioxide.

CLINICAL PHARMACOLOGY

Nifedipine is a calcium ion influx inhibitor (slow-channel blocker or calcium ion antagonist) which inhibits the transmembrane influx of calcium ions into vascular smooth muscle and cardiac muscle. The contractile processes of vascular smooth muscle and cardiac muscle are dependent upon the movement of extracellular calcium ions into these cells through specific ion channels. Nifedipine selectively inhibits calcium ion influx across the cell membrane of vascular smooth muscle and cardiac muscle without altering serum calcium concentrations.

Mechanism of Action: The mechanism by which nifedipine reduces arterial blood pressure involves peripheral arterial vasodilatation and consequently, a reduction in peripheral vascular resistance. The increased peripheral vascular resistance that is an underlying cause of hypertension results from an increase in active tension in the vascular smooth muscle. Studies have demonstrated that the increase in active tension reflects an increase in cytosolic free calcium.

Nifedipine is a peripheral arterial vasodilator which acts directly on vascular smooth muscle. The binding of nifedipine to voltage-dependent and possibly receptor-operated channels in vascular smooth muscle results in an inhibition of calcium influx through these channels. Stores of intracellular calcium in vascular smooth muscle are limited and thus dependent upon the influx of extracellular calcium for contraction to occur. The reduction in calcium influx by nifedipine causes arterial vasodilation and decreased peripheral vascular resistance which results in reduced arterial blood pressure.

Pharmacokinetics and Metabolism: Nifedipine is completely absorbed after oral administration. The bioavailability of nifedipine as ADALAT CC relative to immediate release nifedipine is in the range of 84%-89%. After ingestion of ADALAT CC tablets under fasting conditions, plasma concentrations peak at about 2.5-5 hours with a second small peak or shoulder evident at approximately 6-12 hours post dose. The elimination half-life of nifedipine administered as ADALAT CC is approximately 7 hours in contrast to the known 2 hour elimination half-life of nifedipine administered as an immediate release capsule.

When ADALAT CC is administered as multiples of 30 mg tablets over a dose range of 30 mg to 90 mg, the area under the curve (AUC) is dose proportional; however, the peak plasma concentration for the 90 mg dose given as 3×30 mg is 29% greater than predicted from the 30 mg and 60 mg doses.

Two 30 mg ADALAT CC tablets may be interchanged with a 60 mg ADALAT CC tablet. Three 30 mg ADALAT CC tablets, however, result in substantially higher C_{max} values than those after a single 90 mg ADALAT CC tablet. Three 30 mg tablets should, therefore, not be considered interchangeable with a 90 mg tablet.

Once daily dosing of ADALAT CC under fasting conditions results in decreased fluctuations in the plasma concentration of nifedipine when compared to t.i.d. dosing with immediate release nifedipine capsules. The mean peak plasma concentration of nifedipine following a 90 mg ADALAT CC tablet, administered under fasting conditions, is approximately 115 ng/mL. When ADALAT CC is given immediately after a high fat meal in healthy volunteers, there is an average increase of 60% in the peak plasma nifedipine concentration, a prolongation in the time to peak concentration, but no significant change in the AUC. Plasma concentrations of nifedipine when ADALAT CC is taken after a fatty meal result in slightly lower peaks compared to the same daily dose of the immediate release formulation administered in three divided doses. This may be, in part, because ADALAT CC is less bioavailable than the immediate release formulation.

Nifedipine is extensively metabolized to highly water soluble, inactive metabolites accounting for 60% to 80% of the dose excreted in the urine. Only traces (less than 0.1% of the dose) of the unchanged form can be detected in the urine. The remainder is excreted in the feces in metabolized form, most likely as a result of biliary excretion.

ADALAT® CC (nifedipine) EXTENDED RELEASE TABLETS

No studies have been performed with ADALAT CC in patients with renal failure; however, significant alterations in the pharmacokinetics of nifedipine immediate release capsules have not been reported in patients undergoing hemodialysis or chronic ambulatory peritoneal dialysis. Since the absorption of nifedipine from ADALAT CC could be modified by renal disease, caution should be exercised in treating such patients.

Because hepatic biotransformation is the predominant route for the disposition of nifedipine, its pharmacokinetics may be altered in patients with chronic liver disease. ADALAT CC has not been studied in patients with hepatic disease; however, in patients with hepatic impairment (liver cirrhosis) nifedipine has a longer elimination half-life and higher bioavailability than in healthy volunteers.

The degree of protein binding of nifedipine is high (92%-98%). Protein binding may be greatly reduced in patients with renal or hepatic impairment.

After administration of ADALAT CC to healthy elderly men and women (age > 60 years), the mean C_{max} is 36% higher and the average plasma concentration is 70% greater than in younger patients.

Clinical Studies: ADALAT CC produced dose-related decreases in systolic and diastolic blood pressure as demonstrated in two double-blind, randomized, placebo-controlled trials in which over 350 patients were treated with ADALAT CC 30, 60 or 90mg once daily for 6 weeks. In the first study, ADALAT CC was given as monotherapy and in the second study, ADALAT CC was added to a beta-blocker in patients not controlled on a beta-blocker alone. The mean trough (24 hours post-dose) blood pressure results from these studies are shown below:

MEAN REDUCTIONS IN TROUGH SUPINE BLOOD PRESSURE (mmHg)
SYSTOLIC/DIASTOLIC

ADALAT CC DOSE	STUDY 1 N	MEAN TROUGH REDUCTION*
30 MG	60	5.3/2.9
60 MG	57	8.0/4.1
90 MG	55	12.5/8.1

ADALAT CC DOSE	STUDY 2 N	MEAN TROUGH REDUCTION*
30 MG	58	7.6/3.8
60 MG	63	10.1/5.3
90 MG	62	10.2/5.8

*Placebo response subtracted.

The trough/peak ratios estimated from 24 hour blood pressure monitoring ranged from 41%-78% for diastolic and 46%-91% for systolic blood pressure.

Hemodynamics: Like other slow-channel blockers, nifedipine exerts a negative inotropic effect on isolated myocardial tissue. This is rarely, if ever, seen in intact animals or man, probably because of reflex responses to its vasodilating effects. In man, nifedipine decreases peripheral vascular resistance which leads to a fall in systolic and diastolic pressures, usually minimal in normotensive volunteers (less than 5-10 mm Hg systolic), but sometimes larger. With ADALAT CC, these decreases in blood pressure are not accompanied by any significant change in heart rate. Hemodynamic studies of the immediate release nifedipine formulation in patients with normal ventricular function have generally found a small increase in cardiac index without major effects on ejection fraction, left ventricular end-diastolic pressure (LVEDP) or volume (LVEDV). In patients with impaired ventricular function, most acute studies have shown some increase in ejection fraction and reduction in left ventricular filling pressure.

Electrophysiologic Effects: Although, like other members of its class, nifedipine causes a slight depression of sinoatrial node function and atrioventricular conduction in isolated myocardial preparations, such effects have not been seen in studies in intact animals or in man. In formal electrophysiologic studies, predominantly in patients with normal conduction systems, nifedipine administered as the immediate release capsule has had no tendency to prolong atrioventricular conduction or sinus node recovery time, or to slow sinus rate.

INDICATION AND USAGE

ADALAT CC is indicated for the treatment of hypertension. It may be used alone or in combination with other antihypertensive agents.

CONTRAINDICATIONS

Known hypersensitivity to nifedipine.

WARNINGS

Excessive Hypotension: Although in most patients the hypotensive effect of nifedipine is modest and well tolerated, occasional patients have had excessive and poorly tolerated hypotension. These responses have usually occurred during initial titration or at the time of subsequent upward dosage adjustment, and may be more likely in patients using concomitant beta-blockers.

Severe hypotension and/or increased fluid volume requirements have been reported in patients who received immediate release capsules together with a beta-blocking agent and who underwent coronary artery bypass surgery using high dose fentanyl anesthesia. The interaction with high dose fentanyl appears to be due to the combination of nifedipine and a beta-blocker, but the possibility that it may occur with nifedipine alone, with low doses of fentanyl, in other surgical procedures, or with other narcotic analgesics cannot be ruled out. In nifedipine-treated patients where surgery using high dose fentanyl anesthesia is contemplated, the physician should be aware of these potential problems and, if the patient's condition permits, sufficient time (at least 36 hours) should be allowed for nifedipine to be washed out of the body prior to surgery.

Increased Angina and/or Myocardial Infarction: Rarely, patients, particularly those who have severe obstructive coronary artery disease, have developed well documented increased frequency, duration and/or severity of angina or acute myocardial infarction upon starting nifedipine or at the time of dosage increase. The mechanism of this effect is not established.

Beta-Blocker Withdrawal: When discontinuing a beta-blocker it is important to taper its dose, if possible, rather than stopping abruptly before beginning nifedipine. Patients recently withdrawn from beta blockers may develop a withdrawal syndrome with increased angina, probably related to increased sensitivity to catecholamines. Initiation of nifedipine treatment will not prevent this occurrence and on occasion has been reported to increase it.

Congestive Heart Failure: Rarely, patients (usually while receiving a beta-blocker) have developed heart failure after beginning nifedipine. Patients with tight aortic stenosis may be at greater risk for such an event, as the unloading effect of nifedipine would be expected to be of less benefit to these patients, owing to their fixed impedance to flow across the aortic valve.

PRECAUTIONS

General - Hypotension: Because nifedipine decreases peripheral vascular resistance, careful monitoring of blood pressure during the initial administration and titration of ADALAT CC is suggested. Close observation is especially recommended for patients already taking medications that are known to lower blood pressure (See WARNINGS).

Peripheral Edema: Mild to moderate peripheral edema occurs in a dose-dependent manner with ADALAT CC. The placebo subtracted rate is approximately 8% at 30 mg, 12% at 60 mg and 19% at 90 mg daily. This edema is a localized phenomenon, thought to be associated with vasodilation of dependent arterioles and small blood vessels and not due to left ventricular dysfunction or generalized fluid retention. With patients whose hypertension is complicated by congestive heart failure, care should be taken to differentiate this peripheral edema from the effects of increasing left ventricular dysfunction.

Information for Patients: ADALAT CC is an extended release tablet and should be swallowed whole and taken on an empty stomach. It should not be administered with food. Do not chew, divide or crush tablets.

Laboratory Tests: Rare, usually transient, but occasionally significant elevations of enzymes such as alkaline phosphatase, CPK, LDH, SGOT, and SGPT have been noted. The relationship to nifedipine therapy is uncertain in most cases, but probable in some. These laboratory abnormalities have rarely been associated with clinical symptoms; however, cholestasis with or without jaundice has been reported. A small increase (<5%) in mean alkaline phosphatase was noted in patients treated with ADALAT CC. This was an isolated finding and it rarely resulted in values which fell outside the normal range. Rare instances of allergic hepatitis have been reported with nifedipine treatment. In controlled studies, ADALAT CC did not adversely affect serum uric acid, glucose, cholesterol or potassium.

Nifedipine, like other calcium channel blockers, decreases platelet aggregation *in vitro*. Limited clinical studies have demonstrated a moderate but statistically significant decrease in platelet aggregation and increase in bleeding time in some nifedipine patients. This is thought to be a function of inhibition of calcium transport across the platelet membrane. No clinical significance for these findings has been demonstrated.

Positive direct Coombs' test with or without hemolytic anemia has been reported but a causal relationship between nifedipine administration and positivity of this laboratory test, including hemolysis, could not be determined.

Although nifedipine has been used safely in patients with renal dysfunction and has been reported to exert a beneficial effect in certain cases, rare reversible elevations in BUN and serum creatinine have been reported in patients with pre-existing chronic renal insufficiency. The relationship to nifedipine therapy is uncertain in most cases but probable in some.

Drug Interactions: Beta-adrenergic blocking agents: (See WARNINGS).

ADALAT CC was well tolerated when administered in combination with a beta blocker in 187 hypertensive patients in a placebo-controlled clinical trial. However, there have been occasional literature reports suggesting that the combination of nifedipine and beta-adrenergic blocking drugs may increase the likelihood of congestive heart failure, severe hypotension, or exacerbation of angina in patients with cardiovascular disease.

Digitalis: Since there have been isolated reports of patients with elevated digoxin levels, and there is a possible interaction between digoxin and ADALAT CC, it is recommended that digoxin levels be monitored when initiating, adjusting, and discontinuing ADALAT CC to avoid possible over- or under-digitalization.

Coumarin Anticoagulants: There have been rare reports of increased prothrombin time in patients taking coumarin anticoagulants to whom nifedipine was administered. However, the relationship to nifedipine therapy is uncertain.

Quinidine: There have been rare reports of an interaction between quinidine and nifedipine (with a decreased plasma level of quinidine).

Cimetidine: Both the peak plasma level of nifedipine and the AUC may increase in the presence of cimetidine. Ranitidine produces smaller non-significant increases. This effect of cimetidine may be mediated by its known inhibition of hepatic cytochrome P-450, the enzyme system probably responsible for the first-pass metabolism of nifedipine. If nifedipine therapy is initiated in a patient currently receiving cimetidine, cautious titration is advised.

Carcinogenesis, Mutagenesis, Impairment of Fertility: Nifedipine was administered orally to rats for two years and was not shown to be carcinogenic. When given to rats prior to mating, nifedipine caused reduced fertility at a dose approximately 30 times the maximum recommended human dose. *In vivo* mutagenicity studies were negative.

Pregnancy: Pregnancy Category C. In rodents, rabbits and monkeys, nifedipine has been shown to have a variety of embryotoxic, placentotoxic and fetotoxic effects, including stunted fetuses (rats, mice and rabbits), digital anomalies (rats and rabbits), rib deformities (mice), cleft palate (mice), small placentas and underdeveloped chorionic villi (monkeys), embryonic and fetal deaths (rats, mice and rabbits), prolonged pregnancy (rats; not evaluated in other species), and decreased neonatal survival (rats; not evaluated in other species). On a mg/kg or mg/m^2 basis, some of the doses associated with these various effects are higher than the maximum recommended human dose and some are lower, but all are within an order of magnitude of it.

The digital anomalies seen in nifedipine-exposed rabbit pups are strikingly similar to those seen in pups exposed to phenytoin, and these are in turn similar to the phalangeal deformities that are the most common malformation seen in human children with *in utero* exposure to phenytoin.

There are no adequate and well-controlled studies in pregnant women. ADALAT CC should be used during pregnancy only if the potential benefit justifies the potential risk to the fetus.

Nursing Mothers: Nifedipine is excreted in human milk. Therefore, a decision should be made to discontinue nursing or to discontinue the drug, taking into account the importance of the drug to the mother.

ADVERSE EXPERIENCES

The incidence of adverse events during treatment with ADALAT CC in doses up to 90 mg daily were derived from multi-center placebo-controlled clinical trials in 370 hypertensive patients. Atenolol 50 mg once daily was used concomitantly in 187 of the 370 patients on ADALAT CC and in 64 of the 126 patients on placebo. All adverse events reported during ADALAT CC therapy were tabulated independently of their causal relationship to medication.

The most common adverse event reported with ADALAT® CC was peripheral edema. This was dose related and the frequency was 18% on ADALAT CC 30 mg daily, 22% on ADALAT CC 60 mg daily and 29% on ADALAT CC 90 mg daily versus 10% on placebo.

Other common adverse events reported in the above placebo-controlled trials include:

Adverse Event	ADALAT CC (%) (n=370)	PLACEBO (%) (n=126)
Headache	19	13
Flushing/heat sensation	4	0
Dizziness	4	2
Fatigue/asthenia	4	4
Nausea	2	1
Constipation	1	0

Where the frequency of adverse events with ADALAT CC and placebo is similar, causal relationship cannot be established.

The following adverse events were reported with an incidence of 3% or less in daily doses up to 90 mg:

Body as a Whole/Systemic: chest pain, leg pain

Central Nervous System: paresthesia, vertigo

Dermatologic: rash

Gastrointestinal: constipation

Musculoskeletal: leg cramps

Respiratory: epistaxis, rhinitis

Urogenital: impotence, urinary frequency

Other adverse events reported with an incidence of less than 1.0% were:

Body as a Whole/Systemic: cellulitis, chills, facial edema, neck pain, pelvic pain, pain

Cardiovascular: atrial fibrillation, bradycardia, cardiac arrest, extrasystole, hypotension, palpitations, phlebitis, postural hypotension, tachycardia, cutaneous angiectases

Central Nervous System: anxiety, confusion, decreased libido, depression, hypertonia, insomnia, somnolence

Dermatologic: pruritus, sweating

Gastrointestinal: abdominal pain, diarrhea, dry mouth, dyspepsia, esophagitis, flatulence, gastrointestinal hemorrhage, vomiting

Hematologic: lymphadenopathy

Metabolic: gout, weight loss

Musculoskeletal: arthralgia, arthritis, myalgia

Respiratory: dyspnea, increased cough, rales, pharyngitis

Special Senses: abnormal vision, amblyopia, conjunctivitis, diplopia, tinnitus

Urogenital/Reproductive: kidney calculus, nocturia, breast engorgement

The following adverse events have been reported rarely in patients given nifedipine in other formulations: allergenic hepatitis, alopecia, anemia, arthritis with ANA (+), depression, erythromelalgia, exfoliative dermatitis, fever, gingival hyperplasia, gynecomastia, leukopenia, mood changes, muscle cramps, nervousness, paranoid syndrome, purpura, shakiness, sleep disturbances, syncope, taste perversion, thrombocytopenia, transient blindness at the peak plasma level, tremor and urticaria.

OVERDOSAGE

Experience with nifedipine overdosage is limited. Generally, overdosage with nifedipine loading to pronounced hypotension calls for active cardiovascular support including monitoring of cardiovascular and respiratory function, elevation of extremities, judicious use of calcium infusion, pressor agents and fluids. Clearance of nifedipine would be expected to be prolonged in patients with impaired liver function. Since nifedipine is highly protein bound, dialysis is not likely to be of any benefit; however, plasmapheresis may be beneficial.

There has been one reported case of massive overdosage with tablets of another extended release formulation of nifedipine. The main effects of ingestion of approximately 4800 mg of nifedipine in a young man attempting suicide as a result of cocaine-induced depression was initial dizziness, palpitations, flushing, and nervousness. Within several hours of ingestion, nausea, vomiting, and generalized edema developed. No significant hypotension was apparent at presentation, 18 hours post ingestion. Blood chemistry abnormalities consisted of a mild, transient elevation of serum creatinine, and modest elevations of LDH and CPK, but normal SGOT. Vital signs remained stable, no electrocardiographic abnormalities were noted and renal function returned to normal within 24 to 48 hours with routine supportive measures alone. No prolonged sequelae were observed.

The effect of a single 900 mg ingestion of nifedipine capsules in a depressed anginal patient on tricyclic antidepressants was loss of consciousness within 30 minutes of ingestion, and profound hypotension, which responded to calcium infusion, pressor agents, and fluid replacement. A variety of ECG abnormalities were seen in this patient with a history of bundle branch block, including sinus bradycardia and varying degrees of AV block. These dictated the prophylactic placement of a temporary ventricular pacemaker, but otherwise resolved spontaneously. Significant hyperglycemia was seen initially in this patient, but plasma glucose levels rapidly normalized without further treatment.

A young hypertensive patient with advanced renal failure ingested 280 mg of nifedipine capsules at one time, with resulting marked hypotension responding to calcium infusion and fluids. No AV conduction abnormalities, arrhythmias, or pronounced changes in heart rate were noted, nor was there any further deterioration in renal function.

DOSAGE AND ADMINISTRATION

Dosage should be adjusted according to each patient's needs. It is recommended that ADALAT CC be administered orally once daily on an empty stomach. ADALAT CC is an extended release dosage form and tablets should be swallowed whole, not bitten or divided. In general, titration should proceed over a 7-14 day period starting with 30 mg once daily. Upward titration should be based on therapeutic efficacy and safety. The usual maintenance dose is 30 mg to 60 mg once daily. Titration to doses above 90 mg daily is not recommended.

If discontinuation of ADALAT CC is necessary, sound clinical practice suggests that the dosage should be decreased gradually with close physician supervision.

Care should be taken when dispensing ADALAT CC to assure that the extended release dosage form has been prescribed.

HOW SUPPLIED

ADALAT CC extended release tablets are supplied as 30 mg, 60 mg, and 90 mg round film coated tablets. The different strengths can be identified as follows:

Strength	Color	Markings
30 mg	Pink	30 on one side and ADALAT CC on the other side
60 mg	Salmon	60 on one side and ADALAT CC on the other side
90 mg	Dark Red	90 on one side and ADALAT CC on the other side

ADALAT® CC Tablets are supplied in:

	Strength	NDC Code
Bottles of 100	30 mg	0026-8841-51
	60 mg	0026-8851-51
	90 mg	0026-8861-51
Unit Dose Packages of 100	30 mg	0026-8841-48
	60 mg	0026-8851-48
	90 mg	0026-8861-48

The tablets should be protected from light and moisture and stored below 86°F (30°C). Dispense in tight, light-resistant containers.

Pharmaceutical Division

Distributed by:
Bayer Corporation
Pharmaceutical Division
400 Morgan Lane
West Haven, CT 06516 USA
Made in Germany

PZ500005   3/95   © 1995 Bayer Corporation   4755